P9-EJU-392

BERRIES

A COUNTRY GARDEN COOKBOOK

BERRIES

A COUNTRY GARDEN COOKBOOK

By Sharon Kramis

Photography by Kathryn Kleinman

CollinsPublishersSanFrancisco

A Division of HarperCollinsPublishers

This book is a collection of summer berry-filled memories.
I dedicate it to the memory of James Beard, who loved a good berry patch.

First published in USA 1994 by Collins Publishers San Francisco
Copyright © 1994 Collins Publishers San Francisco
Recipes and text copyright © 1994 Sharon Kramis
Photographs copyright © 1994 Kathryn Kleinman
Food Stylist: Stephanie Greenleigh
Floral and Prop Stylist: Michaele Thunen
Project Direction, Art Direction and Design: Jennifer Barry
Editor: Meesha Halm
The recipe on page 53 is from Oregon's Cuisine of the Rain—From Lush Farm
Foods to Regional Recipes *by Karen Brooks. Copyright © 1993 by Karen Brooks.*
Reprinted with the permission of Addison-Wesley Publishing Company.
Library of Congress Cataloging-in-Publication Data
Kramis, Sharon.
Berries: a country garden cookbook / by Sharon Kramis:
photography by Kathryn Kleinman.
p.   cm.
Includes index.
ISBN 0-00-255344-9
1. Cookery (Berries)   I. Title.
TX813.B4K73 1994
641.6'47--dc20   CIP 93-35624
All rights reserved, including the right of reproduction in whole
or in part or in any form.
Printed in China   10 9 8 7 6 5 4 3 2 1

Acknowledgments
I want to thank the many people who helped me put this book together: my good friend Sally Brown, who worked diligently with me on every step of this project and gave me tremendous support; the great ladies of the food world, Maggie Waldron and Marion Cunningham—thank you for your friendship, your style, your humor and your leadership; Meesha Halm, who was such a good editor— thank you for being patient, understanding, interpretive and such a pleasure to work with; and the berry farmers— hats off to them for the treasures they provide for us. Also thanks to Bill Richter of Richter Berry Farms in Puyallup, Washington; Granger Berry Patch in Granger, Washington; and Berryworks in Corvallis, Oregon. Finally, a
special thank you to "the taster" who has kept a spoon in his hand for the past 30 years and to my very supportive family and friends.

Collins and the photography team would also like to thank Terry Greene, photo assistant; Laura Jerrard, food styling assistant; Kristen Wurz, design and production coordinator; and Jonathan Mills, production manager. Thanks also to Helie Robertson and Barbara, Spencer and Lindsey Hoopes, location; Susan and Hans Nehme, Annette & Company: The Pavillion Antiques; and Betty Jane Roth, props; Carmen Kozlowski and Kozlowski Berry Farm; and Eric Lafko of The Rocky Mountain Jam Company. Special thanks to Michele Miller, Ed Haverty and Michael Schwab.

CONTENTS

INTRODUCTION

It's June, school is out for the summer and strawberries signal the beginning of berry season. I pack a picnic lunch, load my family in the car and head to the U-pick fields 30 miles away. I caution everyone not to pick as many berries as last year, reminding them how long it took me to clean and make jam out of last year's batch. I say this every year, and every year when we reach the fields, the berries are such a bright red and so good to eat, we end up picking more than we can possibly eat in a year's time. Two hours later we carry our berry flats to the weighing stand, pay up and drive off. Dusty and berry-stained, we head for our favorite picnic spot to stretch out on the grass. Those berries not already eaten are tucked away in their coolers. When we arrive home in the evening, everyone disappears while I begin to sort and clean the berries. I slice them for freezing, and with the others I make jam, alternatively tossing one in the pot, one in my mouth. The doors are open, the kitchen is warm and sticky and the baseball game is on. As midnight approaches, I promise myself that next year we won't pick so many berries.

Bowls of berries, baskets of berries, fields of berries— the summer brings us a bounty of berries and happily we eat them all. We eat them fresh or cook them into pies, cobblers and jams. They are intertwined with memories and occasions throughout the summer: Fourth of July means strawberry shortcake, Labor Day brings blueberry cobbler and birthdays and gatherings in between mean lots of berry pies.

My best friend's father loved to pick wild blackberries. It was his hobby and he took it quite seriously, even though the season lasted only 2 to 3 weeks. He had a favorite patch, though he never told anyone where it was. He would take a clean 2-pound shortening can, punch 2 holes in it and attach a wire handle. He'd set out in the morning to patiently gather enough of these jewel-like berries to make a pie. Back at the house he would oversee the cleaning of the berries, coaching his young daughter all the while, "Just a slight drizzle of water when you wash—if you use too much you'll wash away the juice!" Patiently the stems were removed, each berry picked clean, and then it would be time to make a pie. The rules for the pies were few but strict: Never use too much flour and never serve them with ice cream. He was a purist.

There is evidence that berries were eaten and savored as long ago as 5,000 B.C. By the early seventeenth century, berries were cultivated in kitchen gardens in England. Strawberries, in particular, were a favorite subject of European artists, who painted them bright red, plump and ready to eat.

In the New World, the variety of wild berries available delighted the early settlers. They found wild strawberries, blueberries, blackberries, gooseberries and cranberries, which they ate both fresh and cooked. The Native Americans taught them how to preserve them by drying them in the sun. High in vitamins and minerals, berries became an important part of their diet.

The invention of canning in the early nineteenth century led to the gradual near elimination of the local grower markets. Farmers could now grow berries in larger quantities for people who could preserve (rather than immediately have to consume) them. The development of the railroads further aided the growth of the commercial berry market. Once limited to selling their goods in close vicinity, farmers were now able to ship larger quantities across greater distances. It was also around this time that plant breeders and botanists began hybridizing new varieties of cultivated berries, improving the size and quality, making them better suited for growing on a commercial scale.

The Gold Rush of 1849 expanded the commercial berry business further. As huge numbers of pioneers flooded the West, horticultural centers on the northern and central coasts of California were established. Later, when the population migrated into the Pacific Northwest, the Willamette Valley in Oregon became a central growing region for strawberries, blackberries, raspberries, gooseberries and currants. These western regions—Hood River, Oregon, and Watsonville, California, in particular—continue to produce some of the finest berries.

Today, we enjoy a wide choice of beautiful berries. Although berries grow best in certain regions in the United States, thanks to refrigerated shipping they can be enjoyed all around the country. In the summer, you can gather berries from your own garden, seek out the nearest U-pick farm, visit a nearby farmers' market or fill your basket at your own secret berry patch.

GLOSSARY

Selecting: Select plump, firm, ripe, juicy berries with full, even color that indicates that they are ready to pick or have just been picked. Look for shiny blackberries. Avoid those that appear dull and shriveled. Avoid strawberries that have green or white shoulders. Blueberries should be plump, firm and even colored. Never buy mushy berries!

Washing: If you feel it is neccessary to wash berries, place in a colander and rinse gently with a spray nozzle, using as little water as possible. Gently roll out onto several layers of paper towels to absorb the excess water. Washing strawberries first and then removing the stems before storing in the refrigerator helps keep them much fresher.

Storing: It is a good idea to take an ice chest when you go shopping for berries, whether it be at the farmers' market or at the nearby U-pick fields. This will ensure that the berries remain fresh until you get home. At home, empty the baskets of berries into a bowl and remove any moldy ones. One bad berry can spoil the whole lot. Transfer the berries to a chilled pottery bowl, cover with plastic wrap and refrigerate until ready to use. If the berries are extremely soft, store them in a dish in a single layer so that they won't be crushed. It is best to use berries within 2 to 3 days, whether it be for jams, freezing or simply eating. Firmer berries such as blueberries, gooseberries and currants can last up to 4 days.

Freezing: Freezing berries ensures that you will have them for year-round use. Choose berries that are in prime shape with no blemishes. Hull or stem so that they are ready to use from the freezer. Frozen berries should be used while still partially frozen for best texture and for minimal juice lost.

To freeze soft berries, such as strawberries, boysenberries, blackberries and raspberries, line a baking sheet with parchment or waxed paper. Arrange the berries on the paper and separate so that the berries won't touch. Place the baking sheet flat in the freezer so that the berries won't roll. After a few hours, when the berries are frozen solid, transfer into freezer bags, pressing out excess air, and return to the freezer.

You can freeze most berries this way, but I find strawberries freeze better when they are washed gently, hulled, sliced and sprinkled lightly with sugar. (When frozen whole, they tend to collapse and discolor when thawed out.) Blueberries, currants and gooseberries are firm enough to bag directly and then freeze. Cranberries can be frozen in the same bags that they come in.

Measurements and Equivalents:
One flat of berries equals approximately 6 pounds
One pound of berries equals approximately 4 cups
One flat of berries will make about:
5 pints regular jam
Enough filling for 3 pies

Many of the berries called for in this book are interchangeable. Try experimenting with similar varieties. For instance, if you can't find huckleberries, try using blueberries instead. Raspberries will work as equally well as cultivated evergreen blackberries. Boysenberries, nectarberries and loganberries are all natural substitutes for one another. Marionberries, olallieberries and tayberries can also be interchanged, although you'll need to add more sugar to the tayberries.

Blackberry:

The blackberry family contains many varieties, each varying in size and flavor but sharing one characteristic—all contain juice-filled drupelets (or sacs) attached to a core-shaped base that doesn't separate when picked. Varieties include:

Cultivated Evergreen Blackberry: Available mid-June to mid-July. Mid-sized, black, shiny berry. Cultivated on farms and in home gardens. Good eaten fresh or cooked into pies and jams.

Western Wild Blackberry: Available from the end of June until the third week in July. A tiny thimble-shaped, elusive blackberry that is very time-consuming to pick, but wonderful for pies, jams and sauces.

Wild Evergreen Blackberry: Available during the month of July. A round and firm, black, shiny berry; not as large as the Himalaya variety. Leaves are very pointed.

Wild Himalaya Blackberry: Available from mid-July through Labor Day. A large, plump, juicy blackberry that can be found everywhere in the Northwest. Good for crisps, cobblers, jellies and syrups.

Blackberry Hybrids:

Boysenberry: Available from mid-July to mid-August. A dark purple, velvety-looking, very large berry up to 1 1/2 inches long with plump juice sacs. Cultivated in the 1930s by Rudolph Boysen in Napa, California. Sweet, slightly tart, very perfumy and juicy. Wonderful to serve fresh with sliced melons or cooked in pies, cobblers, sauces, jams or syrups.

Loganberry: Available from mid-June to mid-July. A deep reddish maroon slightly cone-shaped, elongated berry, approximately 2 inches long. A blackberry-raspberry cross cultivated in 1881 by Judge Logan of Santa Cruz, California. Full flavored, sweet, with a puckery tart finish. A very juicy berry, it is grown commercially for its juice. Great for making pies, cobblers, jams or simply eating fresh.

Marionberry: Available mid-July to mid-August. A bright, deep black-maroon, medium to large, elongated, cone-shaped berry. A wild-domestic blackberry cross cultivated in 1956 by George F. Waldo in Marion County, Oregon. Excellent flavor with a perfect balance of sweet and tart. Superior for pies, ice creams, jams, jellies and eating fresh.

Nectarberry: Available from mid-July to mid-August. A deep burgundy, jumbo-sized berry, even larger than the boysenberry, which it resembles. Sweet, full of juice, with a slightly floral taste. Excellent eaten fresh, also makes a beautiful jam.

Olallieberry: Available from mid-June to mid-July. A long, slender, firm berry with long juice sacs and shiny black color. A cultivated blackberry cross also developed by George F. Waldo. This berry is grown extensively in Watsonville, California. Well-balanced flavor, a good all-purpose berry, wonderful for pies, cobblers and jams, that freezes beautifully.

Tayberry: Available from mid-June to mid-July. A scarlet red, slightly cone-shaped berry, approximately 1 1/4 inches long. A relative newcomer, this blackberry-raspberry cross was bred in 1977 in Scotland. Tart when eaten fresh, it asserts itself fully when cooked. Works well when mixed with other berries for ice cream, cobblers or pies. It also makes a beautifully colored sauce or syrup (be sure to add a little extra sugar when cooking).

Blueberry:

Available from mid-July to September. A dark blue, smooth, round berry with a slight powdery bloom. Size varies from pea-size to 5/8 inch in diameter. Wild blueberries grow on low bushes in the coastal mountain regions. More than 50 varieties of blueberries are cultivated in the Northwest. Each variety has different flavor characteristics. Taste and identify your favorite. Delicious eaten fresh with a little cream or sprinkled into a fruit salad. Excellent when baked in coffee cakes or muffins.

Cranberry:

Harvested in October; available fresh through December. A round, crimson-colored, firm berry grown in the Northwest and Cape Cod, primarily in cultivated bogs. Also grown in New Jersey and Wisconsin. Called "craneberries" by the early settlers because the flower stamens form a "beak" resembling a crane. Tart and pulpy inside when fresh. Most cranberry recipes require cooking and call for adding sugar. It turns soft and juicy when cooked and adds a pleasant tart flavor to baked goods. The sugared and dried cranberry is wonderful for cookies, scones and sauces.

Currants:

Black Currant: Available from the end of June to mid-July. Round black berry, larger than the red currant. Grows as a single berry rather than in clumps, with fuzzy ends that need to be snipped off before using. More savory than sweet, it is best when cooked. Excellent for sauces to accompany pork, chicken and wild game. Used to make crème de cassis, syrups and preserves.

Red Currant: Available from the end of June to mid-July. Small, round, bright red berry with a transparent look. Grows on a bush in clumps like grapes. Tart and juicy. Excellent as a fresh garnish, often used for jellies and sauces. Once very popular, today the red currant is available at some farmers' markets, but difficult to find elsewhere.

White Currant: Available from the end of June to mid-July. A small, round white berry that looks like a transparent pearl. Grows in clumps like the red currant. Sweeter than the red currant, it has a wonderful flavor. Ideal eaten fresh along with a crisp sugar cookie and a dish of vanilla ice cream. It is an unusual and delicious edible garnish for desserts and entrées.

Gooseberry:

Available from late June to mid-July. Slightly transparent light jade- or rose-colored berry with thick skin ranging from pea-size to large marble-size. It's brown fuzzy ends need to be removed before cooking. Ranges in flavor from very tart to sweet. Can be eaten fresh, but more commonly used in sauces, puddings, jams and pies.

Blackberries

Blueberries

Currants

Cranberries

Boysenberries

Huckleberries

Gooseberries

Lingonberries

Marionberries

Loganberries

Strawberries

Black Raspberries

Golden Raspberries

Olallieberries

Red Raspberries

Tayberries

Huckleberries:

Blue Huckleberry: Available from mid-June through Labor Day. Small round blueberry that has a delicious flavor. Often identified incorrectly as a blueberry. Found growing wild in the lower mountains.

European Huckleberry: Available from mid-June through Labor Day. A small, purplish red berry that crunches when you eat it. It makes wonderful crimson-colored syrups and jams and is the perfect addition to pancakes. Found growing wild.

Wild Red Huckleberry: Available from mid-June through Labor Day. Tiny red berry with delicate green foliage. Often used by florists, it is fun to just pop the berries in your mouth as you walk along through the woods where they grow wild.

Lingonberry:

Available late August and September. Bright red, small round berry. Similar in taste to a cranberry, but not as tart. Common in Scandinavia where it grows wild so abundantly. Available in limited quantities in Alaska. Related to the cranberry, it is a low-growing evergreen plant. Most commonly used for syrups and jams.

Raspberries:

Black Raspberry (also called Blackcaps): Available from July 1 to July 21. Dark, purplish black, small, seedy, thimble-shaped berry that separates from the center core when picked. A unique flavor that tastes almost more savory than sweet. Popular in jams and ice creams because of its vibrant color. Excellent in a cooked sauce for meat dishes, not as good for eating fresh.

Golden Raspberry: Available during the month of July in limited quantities. A golden yellow, soft berry that separates from the center core when picked. Cap-shaped, it is smaller than the red variety. Although it is dry looking, it is surprisingly juicy and sweet. Best when eaten fresh. Looks wonderful on top of desserts or as a garnish alongside grilled fish.

Red Raspberry: Available from mid-June to mid-July. A second crop of red raspberries are harvested from mid-August to mid-September in limited quantities. Deep red, elongated, thimble-shaped berry that is best when picked and eaten fresh. Wonderful with a little cream, on top of tarts and cakes, or cooked in jam or pies.

Strawberries:

Cultivated Strawberry: Available from the beginning of June to mid-July. Bright flame-red to deep scarlet color. A small to jumbo, heart-shaped berry. It can be either very sweet and flavorful or disappointing. The most flavorful are the local varieties, which are sweeter and juicier and haven't been bred for shipping. Best eaten fresh on shortcakes or incorporated in ice cream or made into jam.

Wild (Alpine) Strawberry: Available from July to September. A tiny, fragrant red or white wild strawberry full of sweet flavor. Though the wild strawberry is not commercially grown, it can be found worldwide growing wild, particularly in the forests. Known as *fraises des bois* ("strawberries of the woods") in France. A low-growing shrub, the wild strawberry bush is popularly used in landscaping.

OPENERS

The first bright red strawberries that appear in your garden signal the onset of summer and the opening of berry season. They are the first act, followed by raspberries, blackberries, blueberries, huckleberries and more—and, in the middle of the summer, they all appear on stage together.

Summer signals that it is time to relax, kick back and enjoy the good life. This is the time to invite good friends over for a light, casual meal to be enjoyed outdoors.

The Chilled Strawberry Soup provides a first course for a simple summer supper. The classic prosciutto and melon appetizer is dressed up by the addition of fresh boysenberries.

Salads get a boost with fresh berries and berry-based dressings. In the Raspberry, Blue Cheese and Toasted Walnut Salad, raspberries are used two ways—raspberry vinegar to make the vinaigrette and fresh raspberries to garnish the salad. Try making a fruit vinegar such as Tayberry Vinegar and see how it changes the nature of your favorite salad.

As summer ends, the season's first cranberries appear. This is a perfect time to put up some jars of Cranberry Orange Apple Relish. This sweet and savory condiment provides just the right zip to Warm Roasted Chicken and Watercress Sandwiches.

Assorted Fruit-Flavored Vinegars

Chilled Strawberry Soup with Pound Cake Croutons

Chilled Strawberry Soup with Pound Cake Croutons

*This is a perfect picnic soup. Pack it
in your thermos to keep it cool and serve it when
you spread your blanket under a big tree.*

4 cups sliced fresh strawberries
1 banana, cut in 4 pieces
1 cup pineapple, orange or banana juice
1 cup light sour cream
1 tablespoon raspberry liqueur
2 ice cubes
1 1/2 cups of pound cake, cut into 1/2-inch cubes
6 sprigs fresh mint, for garnish

In a food processor or blender, process the strawberries, banana, juice, sour cream and liqueur until smooth.

Add the ice cubes and swirl briefly to chill the liquid. Remove the ice cubes before they melt completely.

Preheat the oven to broil. Place the pound cake cubes onto a baking sheet. Toast for 6 minutes under broiler, turning once to brown on 2 sides.

To serve, pour the soup into small, chilled bowls and garnish with the toasted pound cake croutons and mint sprigs. *Serves 6*

Skewers of Honeydew, Prosciutto and Boysenberries

*This starter mingles the flavors of the sweet
melon, salty cured ham and wine-like boysenberry.
The color contrasts mean a visual treat as well.*

1/2 ripe honeydew melon
1/4 pound prosciutto, very thinly sliced,
    then cut into 1 1/2-inch ribbons
6 fresh mint leaves
6 large fresh boysenberries (or strawberries)
Freshly ground black pepper, to taste

Scoop out the seeds of the melon and place skin-side up on cutting board. Following the curve of the melon with a sharp knife, cut downward, removing the tough skin. Cut into 1 1/2-inch cubes.

Thread 1 cube of honeydew on a 6-inch bamboo skewer, followed with a prosciutto ribbon gathered onto the skewer in an "S" shape, another honeydew cube, a flat mint leaf and a large boysenberry. Repeat until all the ingredients are skewered.

To serve, place the finished skewers on a round serving platter in starburst fashion and top with freshly ground black pepper. *Serves 6*

Summer Fruit Bowl with Just-Picked Berries

Summer Fruit Bowl with Just-Picked Berries

There's nothing more appealing in the summer than a beautiful bowl of chilled fresh fruit. The bright colors and flavors of strawberries, blueberries and fresh melons blend together so well.

1/4 large watermelon
1 cantaloupe
1 honeydew melon
Juice of 1 lime
1/4 cup chilled champagne, soda water or 7-Up
1 1/2 cups green seedless grapes
1 1/2 cups red seedless grapes
4 cups strawberries, hulled and halved
1 cup blueberries

Remove the skins and seeds of the melons and cut into bite-sized pieces. Or shape into rounds using a melon baller. Place melon balls in a large glass bowl, cover with plastic wrap and chill for at least 2 hours.

Just before serving, drizzle with the fresh lime juice and champagne (or other sparkling drink). Add the grapes, strawberries and blueberries. Toss very gently. *Serves 6 to 8*

Strawberry Spinach Salad with Toasted Almonds

This is the salad that everybody wants the recipe for. Whenever I make it, there's never a single spinach leaf left in the bowl.

2 bunches fresh spinach, washed, trimmed and
    well dried
1/2 cup slivered almonds

Dressing:
1/2 cup orange juice concentrate (undiluted)
1/2 cup mayonnaise

2 cups fresh strawberries, hulled and sliced

Tear the spinach leaves into bite-sized pieces and place in a glass bowl. Cover with plastic wrap and chill.

Preheat the oven to 350 degrees F. Place the almonds in a shallow pan and toast for 15 minutes. Let cool.

Whisk the orange juice concentrate and mayonnaise together until well blended.

To serve, pour the dressing over the spinach and turn until well coated. Sprinkle with the strawberries and almonds. *Serves 6*

Tayberry Vinegar

The tayberry is a large, very tart red berry similar in shape to the boysenberry. You can use wild blackberries, boysenberries or marionberries to make other fruit-flavored vinegars. They make excellent gifts and give new vitality to summer salads.

2 cups fresh tayberries (or another berry
of your choice), left whole
1/2 cup granulated sugar
4 cups distilled white vinegar
Sprigs of fresh herbs or fresh edible flowers (optional)

Use a single berry variety for each vinegar recipe. For the clearest vinegar, do not mix berries. Place the berries, sugar and vinegar in a 1-quart glass jar. Store in a cool, dark place for 3 weeks.

Carefully strain into 4 half-pint bottles. Discard the pulp and seeds. At this point, you can add edible flowers or complementary herbs such as mint leaves for visual interest, if desired. Cap the bottles and keep refrigerated. Vinegar will last up to 3 months in the refrigerator. *Makes 4 half-pints*

Note: Most berries will bleach in the vinegar, but fresh cranberries can be threaded on bamboo skewers with garlic cloves and will retain their color.

Raspberries, Blue Cheese and Toasted Walnut Salad

In the summer, the farmers' markets bring a variety of baby greens that are delicious tossed with a raspberry vinaigrette and sprinkled with the different textures of crisp walnuts, creamy blue cheese and tart berries.

Raspberry Vinaigrette:
2 shallots, finely chopped
1 tablespoon Dijon mustard
1/4 cup raspberry vinegar
2 tablespoons balsamic vinegar
2 tablespoons honey
2 tablespoons fresh orange juice
1 cup olive oil

1/2 cup walnuts
4 cups assorted baby greens (such as lollo rossa,
red butter, curly endive, Tom Thumb,
red oak leaf or radicchio), washed and dried
2 ounces blue cheese, crumbled
1 cup fresh raspberries

In a medium bowl, combine the shallots and mustard with the vinegars. Add the honey and orange juice and whisk to blend. Drizzle in the olive oil and whisk until blended. *Makes 1 3/4 cups of vinaigrette*

Preheat the oven to 350 degrees F. Place the walnuts in a shallow pan and toast for 15 minutes. Let cool and roughly chop.

In a large salad bowl, toss the baby greens with 1/2 cup of the raspberry vinaigrette, or to taste. Divide the greens on 4 plates and top with crumbled blue cheese, fresh raspberries and toasted walnuts. *Serves 4*

Warm Roasted Chicken and Watercress Sandwiches with Cranberry Orange Apple Relish

This relish is the perfect condiment for a warm roasted chicken sandwich.
You can eat the relish alongside the sandwich or spread it on the bread.

Cranberry Orange Apple Relish:
1 pound (4 cups) cranberries
2 Granny Smith apples, cored and coarsely chopped
2 oranges, peel on, quartered and coarsely chopped
2 cups granulated sugar

1 medium roasting chicken,
*   approximately 3 to 4 pounds*
Salt and freshly ground black pepper, to taste
1/4 cup olive oil
1 tablespoon lemon zest, julienned
Juice of 1 lemon, strained

4 teaspoons fresh thyme (or 2 teaspoons dried thyme)
2 teaspoons fresh rosemary (or 1 teaspoon
*   crushed dried rosemary)*
1 teaspoon fresh marjoram (or 1/2 teaspoon
*   dried marjoram)*
2 cloves garlic, finely chopped
1/2 cup small green Greek olives (optional)

1 French baguette, sliced into 8 pieces and split open
Mayonnaise, to taste
Unsalted butter, to taste
Watercress sprigs

To prepare the cranberry orange apple relish, place the cranberries in the bowl of a food processor and process until finely chopped. Transfer to a medium bowl.

Process the apples and then the oranges, each time turning chopped fruit into the bowl with the chopped cranberries. Add the sugar to the fruit and mix well. Refrigerate for several hours. The relish can be frozen or stored in the refrigerator for up to 4 weeks. *Makes approximately 5 cups*

Preheat the oven to 450 degrees F.

Rub the exterior of the chicken with salt and pepper. In a small bowl, combine the olive oil, lemon zest and juice, herbs, garlic and a bit more pepper. Brush the chicken generously with the marinade, inside and out.

Place chicken on a roasting rack in a roasting pan. Pour the remaining marinade over the chicken. Add 1 cup water to the roasting pan. Place pan in the oven and reduce heat to 350 degrees F.

Bake for 1 to 1 1/2 hours, basting chicken with pan juices every 20 minutes, until meat is tender. Add the olives to the roasting pan, if you wish, during the last 30 minutes of cooking time.

To prepare the sandwiches, spread some mayonnaise on one side of a slice of baguette, and some butter on the other side. Pull off the meat from roasted chicken, place on the buttered bread and top with peppery sprigs of watercress and relish. The olives can be eaten alongside the sandwich. *Makes 8 sandwiches*

ACCOMPANIMENTS

In the middle of July, when the berry season is in full force, I prefer to eat as many fresh berries as I can. But they don't last for long, so I always find myself putting up jams for the winter months. Standing over my stove cooking jams gives me much pleasure. Carefully stirring the bubbling fruit, pouring it into jars, standing back to survey the finished product and congratulating myself on a job well done is a delightful process. The best part, though, is spreading the freshly made jam on a piece of warm buttered toast.

Jam making is something that has always held a certain amount of intimidation for many cooks; however, my mother, Elsie Mahan, has helped me overcome this with her simple but specific instructions. Her jams are consistently wonderful, bright colored and delicious, capturing the essence of fresh fruit and summer flavors. Remember, when making jam, be sure to gather all the equipment and ingredients in the work area and make sure the work area is spotless.

Next time you have guests over for brunch, try setting the table with an assortment of jams and baked goods. They can make a whole meal.

Clockwise from the back left: Strawberry Jam (recipe p. 32), two jars of Raspberry Plum Jam (recipe p. 33), Red Raspberry Jam (recipe p. 33) and Ollalieberry Jam (recipe p. 33).

Basic Master Strawberry Jam

*This recipe uses a short-boil method with liquid pectin because
it offers greater ease of preparation than powdered pectin. Liquid pectin
requires minimal stirring while the jam is boiling.*

Suggested Equipment:
*8-quart, heavy-bottomed, stainless steel or
   copper-clad kettle*
1- and 2-cup measuring cups
4-cup measuring bowl
1 large bowl
1 long-handled wooden spoon
1 set of measuring spoons
1 long-handled metal spoon
Hot pads or gloves, and cotton towels
Tongs, knife, scissors and cup

1-quart pan, for sterilizing lids
Food processor
Timer or clock

Strawberry Jam Ingredients:
7 half-pint jars and matching lids (use new lids only)
*4 cups crushed strawberries (approximately 6 cups
   whole strawberries)*
7 level cups granulated sugar
1/2 teaspoon margarine
*One 3-ounce pouch liquid pectin (available in
   grocery stores)*

To sterilize the jars, wash and rinse them in the dishwasher without detergent and keep warm under cloth towels. Put lids in a small pan, cover with water and boil for 10 minutes. Turn off heat but keep the lids warm.

Rinse strawberries lightly, but do not bruise. Drain. Completely cut away the green caps and any damaged portions of fruit. Place a small amount of strawberries at a time in a food processor and pulse briefly, making sure to crush but not purée the berries. Repeat until all the strawberries are crushed.

Measure 4 cups of crushed strawberries. Place strawberries and sugar in a large kettle and mix thoroughly.

Open the liquid pectin pouch with scissors. Stand it upright in a cup while waiting for berries to boil. Bring strawberry mixture to a full, rolling boil over high heat. Add the margarine and continue to stir as it melts. Pour in the pectin all at once, stirring vigorously. When mixture reaches a full, rolling boil again, stir for 1 minute.

Remove the kettle from the heat. Set in the sink and, using a metal spoon, skim off any foam. Transfer back to the stove or counter.

With a 1-cup measuring cup or ladle, fill jars with jam up to 1/8 inch from the rim. With a damp cloth, wipe the jar rims. (The rims of jars must be impeccably clean or they will not seal properly.) Quickly place lids on top and screw on tightly. Set the jars upside down on a dry towel. Cover and let stand for 5 minutes. Return to upright position. Cover with large cloth towel and set aside to cool for 8 to 15 hours. Store in a cool, dark place for up to a year. Keep in the refrigerator once opened. *Makes 7 1/2 half-pints of jam*

Red Raspberry Jam

Follow the Basic Master Strawberry Jam recipe except: Use 6 1/2 cups of granulated sugar to 4 cups crushed red raspberries. *Makes 7 half-pints of jam*

Olallieberry Jam

Follow the Basic Master Strawberry Jam recipe except: Use 7 1/2 cups of granulated sugar to 4 cups crushed olallieberries. *Makes 7 1/2 half-pints of jam*

Raspberry Plum Jam

This delicious blend of fruits combines two summer flavors beautifully.

12 half-pint jars and lids
2 1/2 pounds firm, ripe plums
3 cups fresh red raspberries or
   20 ounces unsweetened frozen raspberries

10 cups granulated sugar
1/2 cup lemon juice
1/2 teaspoon margarine
Two 3-ounce pouches liquid pectin

Sterilize the 12 half-pint canning jars and 12 lids, following the directions in Basic Master Strawberry Jam recipe.

Rinse the plums, cut in half and remove pits. Transfer to a bowl in a food processor and chop finely. This should yield 4 cups.

Place the plums and red raspberries in an 8-quart kettle. Add the sugar and lemon juice and stir with a wooden spoon until well mixed.

Open the liquid pectin pouch with scissors. Stand upright in a cup while waiting for berries to boil. Bring the raspberry and plum mixture to a full, rolling boil over high heat. Add the margarine and continue to stir as it melts. Pour in the pectin all at once, stirring vigorously. When the mixture reaches a full, rolling boil again, stir for 1 minute.

Remove the kettle from the heat. Set in the sink and, using a metal spoon, skim off any foam. Transfer back to the stove or counter.

With a 1-cup measuring cup or ladle, fill jars with jam up to 1/8 inch from the rim. With a damp cloth, wipe the jar rims clean. (The rims of jars must be impeccably clean or they will not seal properly.)

Quickly place lids on top and screw on tightly. Set the jars upside down on a dry towel. Cover and let stand for 5 minutes. Return to upright position. Cover with large cloth towel and set aside to cool for 8 to 15 hours. Store in a cool, dark place for up to a year. Keep in the refrigerator once opened. *Makes 12 half-pints of jam*

Swedish Pancakes

These delicate pancakes served with lingonberry preserves are a traditional Scandinavian treat.

3 eggs
2 cups half-and-half
1 cup all-purpose flour
6 tablespoons unsalted butter, melted
1/2 teaspoon salt
1 tablespoon vegetable oil, for greasing the pan

In a large bowl, beat the eggs with 1/2 cup of half-and-half for 3 minutes with an electric mixer or whisk. Add the flour and beat to a heavy, smooth consistency. Beat in the remaining half-and-half until blended, then beat in the melted butter and salt.

Lightly grease a heavy cast-iron skillet or pancake griddle with oil. Heat the skillet until very hot, then pour in the batter. Use approximately 1 tablespoon of batter for each pancake. Each should form a 3-inch circle. Cook 4 pancakes at a time, over medium heat. After about 1 minute, or when the edges brown slightly, flip the pancakes with a spatula and cook for another 1 to 2 minutes. Serve with 1 or more of the lingonberry toppings (see right). *Makes 18 pancakes*

Lingonberry Toppings

Lingonberry preserves can also be folded into whipped cream or butter for delicious variations.

Lingonberry Preserves:
1 pound lingonberries, frozen or fresh
1/2 cup water
1 cup granulated sugar
Clean and rinse the berries. Bring berries and water to a boil in a large saucepan over medium heat. Remove from heat and stir in the sugar. Stir occasionally until preserves are cool. Skim the foam from the preserves with a large metal spoon, then pour into pint-sized jars and refrigerate for up to 2 weeks. Or freeze in a plastic container for up to 1 year. Serve preserves at room temperature. *Makes 1 1/2 pints*

Lingonberry Butter:
1 stick unsalted butter, softened
3 tablespoons lingonberry preserves
Beat the softened butter until smooth. Mix in the lingonberry preserves and serve.

Lingonberry Cream:
4 tablespoons lingonberry preserves
1 cup whipped cream
Fold the lingonberry preserves into the whipped cream and serve.

Lingonberry Sauce:
Stir 1 cup of lingonberry preserves vigorously until it is soft enough to spoon over pancakes.

Lemon-Glazed Huckleberry Muffins

*I've found that the old standard "muffin method"
using vegetable oil produces muffins with the best texture.
These muffins call for tart, plump huckleberries,
but you can use blueberries instead.*

1/2 cup corn oil
2 eggs
1 cup granulated sugar
1 tablespoon lemon zest
2 tablespoons fresh lemon juice
1 3/4 cups all-purpose flour
2 teaspoons baking powder

1/2 teaspoon baking soda
1/2 teaspoon salt
1 1/2 cups huckleberries

Lemon Glaze:
1/4 cup powdered sugar
2 teaspoons lemon zest
2 tablespoons lemon juice

Preheat the oven to 375 degrees F.

In a large bowl with an electric mixer, beat the corn oil and eggs until well blended. Add the sugar and continue beating for 2 minutes or until the mixture is creamy. Add lemon zest and lemon juice.

In a small bowl, combine the flour, baking powder, baking soda and salt. Using a wooden spoon, stir all dry ingredients into the creamy mixture. Be careful not to overmix.

Gently fold in the huckleberries, using a rubber spatula. Grease a 12-cup muffin tin or line the tin with paper muffin cups. Spoon the batter into cups until they are three-quarters full. Bake in the oven for 25 minutes or until muffins are golden brown.

While muffins are baking, prepare the lemon glaze. In a small bowl, combine the powdered sugar, lemon zest and lemon juice. Stir and set aside.

Remove muffins from the oven and pierce each muffin 6 to 8 times with a skewer. Spoon the lemon glaze over the muffins while they are still warm.
Makes 12 muffins

Buttermilk Breakfast Scones with Dried Cranberries

These tender, traditional scones are updated with dried cranberries. They are delicious served warm with cranberry butter.

3 cups unbleached all-purpose flour
1/3 cup granulated sugar
2 1/2 teaspoons baking powder
1/2 teaspoon baking soda
3/4 teaspoon salt
1 1/2 sticks chilled margarine, cut into 6 to 8 pieces
3/4 cup dried cranberries
1 teaspoon grated orange zest
1 cup buttermilk

Glaze:
1 tablespoon cream
1/4 teaspoon ground cinnamon
2 tablespoons granulated sugar

Preheat the oven to 400 degrees F.

In a large bowl, stir the flour, sugar, baking powder, baking soda and salt. Add the margarine and beat with an electric mixer until well blended. Add the dried cranberries and orange zest. Pour in buttermilk and mix until blended.

Gather the dough into a ball and divide in half. On a lightly floured board, roll into 2 circles, approximately 1/2- to 3/4-inch thick. Cut each circle into 8 wedges.

In a small bowl, combine the cream, cinnamon and sugar. Set aside.

Bake scones on lightly greased baking sheet for 12 to 15 minutes, or until scones are golden. Remove scones from the oven and brush with the glaze. *Makes 16 scones*

Cranberry Butter

This delightful compound butter is from Nanci Main and Jimella Lucas, chefs and owners of The Ark Restaurant in Nahcotta, Washington, near the western capital of cranberries. The sweet-tart combination is perfect on scones, muffins, waffles and pancakes as well.

4 sticks unsalted butter, at room temperature
1/2 cup cranberries, coarsely chopped (if frozen, chop them frozen and let thaw)
1/4 cup light brown sugar
1/4 cup honey
4 tablespoons ground walnuts
1/2 cup cranberry sauce*
1 tablespoon grated orange zest
1 teaspoon grated lemon zest
2 tablespoons buttermilk

Place the softened butter in a large bowl and whip at high speed with an electric mixer until it turns pale yellow, scraping the sides of the bowl to make sure all the butter gets whipped.

Add the coarsely chopped cranberries, brown sugar, honey, ground walnuts, cranberry sauce and orange and lemon zests.

Whip at medium speed until the mixture turns light pink.

Add the buttermilk and whip until incorporated. *Makes approximately 1 1/3 pounds*

*Note: If using commercial whole cranberry sauce, empty the can into a small bowl, stir to loosen the sauce, and then measure.

Strawberry Grapefruit Mint Compote

*The tart flavor of the grapefruit balances well with the sweetness
of the fresh strawberries and mint to make a refreshing light dessert or a perfect
prelude to brunch. This is especially pretty in small cut-glass dishes.*

1 large grapefruit
1 cup strawberries, hulled and halved

2 teaspoons granulated sugar
1 teaspoon roughly chopped fresh mint leaves

Cut the top and bottom off grapefruit. With a sharp knife, cut away all peel and pith from outside of whole grapefruit. Then, angle the knife to cut toward the center of the fruit, following section lines, to produce delicate segments without any skin or pith.

In a medium mixing bowl, gently mix the grapefruit segments, strawberries, sugar and mint together. Refrigerate for 1 to 2 hours. *Serves 4*

Blueberry Banana Muffins

These moist muffins are full of plump, juicy blueberries with a background flavor of banana. It's important not to stir the batter too much after you add the flour or they will be rubbery.

1 stick margarine
3/4 cup granulated sugar
2 eggs
2 to 3 bananas, mashed (approximately 1 cup)
1/2 cup milk
2 cups all-purpose flour
2 teaspoons baking powder
1/2 teaspoon ground cinnamon
2 cups fresh or frozen blueberries

Preheat the oven to 375 degrees F.

In a medium bowl with an electric mixer, cream the margarine and sugar. Add the eggs, one at a time. Mix in the bananas and milk.

In another mixing bowl, combine the flour, baking powder and cinnamon. Add the margarine mixture to the dry ingredients and mix only until the batter is moist.

Carefully stir in the whole blueberries. If you are using frozen blueberries, add them to your recipe while they are still frozen or they will turn your batter purple. Spoon the batter into greased muffin cups or use paper muffin-cup liners, filling the cups to the top. Bake in the oven for 30 to 35 minutes or until muffins are golden brown.

Let cool for 5 minutes in the muffin pan, then transfer to a cooling rack. The muffins can be stored in a tightly sealed plastic container or in plastic bags.
Makes 1 dozen muffins

Left to right: Prizewinning Orange Scones with Berries and Cream (recipe p. 45) and Blueberry Banana Muffins

Prizewinning Orange Scones with Berries and Cream

*This is one of our favorite ways to serve fresh berries for brunch or
dessert in the middle of the summer, when all of the berries are ripe at the same time.
They are delicious, even if you only use strawberries.*

Scones:

2 cups sifted all-purpose flour
1 tablespoon baking powder
1 teaspoon salt
2 tablespoons granulated sugar
5 1/2 tablespoons unsalted butter
1 extra large egg, beaten
1/2 cup whipping cream
2 tablespoons unsalted butter, melted
1/2 cup granulated sugar
1 tablespoon orange zest

*6 to 8 cups fresh berries (such as strawberries,
    raspberries, blackberries and tayberries),
    washed and dried*
*3/4 to 1 cup granulated sugar,
    depending upon berry sweetness*
*1 to 1 1/2 cups whipping cream, whipped
    and lightly sweetened with 2 teaspoons
    granulated sugar*

Preheat the oven to 425 degrees F.

In a small bowl, stir together the flour, baking powder, salt and sugar. Add the butter, cutting it into dry ingredients using a pastry blender or 2 knives. In a small bowl, combine the beaten egg and cream and add to the flour mixture. Mix until just blended together.

Turn out the batter onto a lightly floured board and knead for 1 minute. Roll dough into a rectangle approximately 4 inches by 8 inches.

Brush the dough with the melted butter. Sprinkle with the sugar and orange zest. Roll up, jelly roll fashion, and seal the long seam by pinching it together lightly with your fingers.

Cut the roll into eight 1-inch-thick slices. Lay slices down sideways on a lightly greased baking sheet and bake for 12 to 15 minutes, or until scones are golden.

Slice the strawberries and place in a large pretty bowl with other whole berries, if available. Sprinkle with sugar and refrigerate for 1 to 2 hours. To serve, heap spoonfuls of berries over a scone and top with freshly whipped cream. *Makes 8 scones*

MAIN COURSES

What works for a main course in the winter can be too heavy for summertime. Easy-to-prepare and fresh ingredients are the essentials for summer recipes. Entrées of seafood, chicken, pork and lamb are all made more appealing with the accent of fresh berries.

Summertime is salad time and the Orzo Pasta Salad with Crab and Currants makes a nice light dinner. Contrary to many pasta salad recipes, this one is good the next day. The currants add a colorful garnish and a sweet-tart flavor.

Grilled fish is complemented nicely with a sprinkle of fresh fruit. Broiled Halibut with Greek Lemon Sauce, Huckleberries and Chives takes advantage of the wild fruit while barbecued salmon gets a lift with a fresh Strawberry, Mint and Cucumber Salsa.

In the Marinated Lamb Steaks with Gooseberry Chutney recipe, the tartness of the chutney counters the richness of the lamb. If you have enough gooseberries, make extra jars of chutney to enjoy in the winter months, when you resort to using your indoor broiler instead of your outdoor grill.

As summer ends and the first rains begin, wild mushrooms start to appear along with the season's first cranberries. These are wonderful together in the Pork Tenderloin with Sautéed Wild Mushrooms, Cranberries, Blueberries and Port.

Orzo Pasta Salad with Crab and Currants

*Crystal Nailor, a chef friend of mine, prepared this pasta salad
for a Saturday lunch gathering and everyone loved it. Even if you aren't
a pasta salad lover, this one will make you come back for more.*

Vinaigrette:
1/2 cup walnut oil
2 cups vegetable oil
1/4 cup balsamic vinegar
1/4 cup red wine vinegar
2 cloves garlic, finely chopped
*4 tablespoons finely chopped fresh thyme or
    2 tablespoons dried thyme*
*4 tablespoons finely chopped fresh basil or
    2 tablespoons dried basil*
Juice of 3 lemons
1 tablespoon freshly ground black pepper

*2 packages orzo pasta (8 ounces each) cooked
    al dente, rinsed and drained well*
*1 to 1 1/2 pounds Dungeness crab meat,
    fresh or frozen*
1/2 cup Kalamata olives, pitted and sliced
2 yellow bell peppers, seeded and finely diced
1 red bell pepper, seeded and finely diced
6 tablespoons capers, rinsed
2 medium tomatoes, coarsely chopped
2 bunches fresh basil, cut into thin strips
1/2 cup feta cheese, crumbled
1 cup red and black currants

To prepare the vinaigrette, whisk together all ingredients in a medium bowl.

In a large salad bowl, place cooked orzo pasta. Add the crab, olives, yellow and red peppers, capers, tomatoes, basil, feta and currants. Toss salad with two-thirds of the vinaigrette, reserving the rest. Chill the dressed salad for at least 2 hours to let the flavors develop. At serving time, check salad for flavor and add more dressing, if necessary. *Serves 8 to 10*

Barbecued Salmon with Strawberry, Mint and Cucumber Salsa

This dish is a family favorite. The texture and flavor of the strawberry and cucumber blend together to make a colorful and flavorful condiment to serve with the grilled salmon.

Strawberry, Mint and Cucumber Salsa:
1 English (or seedless) cucumber, finely chopped
1 green onion, thinly sliced
1 tablespoon fresh mint, cut into thin strips
3 to 4 tablespoons seasoned rice wine vinegar
2 cups fresh strawberries, hulled and finely diced

Barbecue Sauce:
1 stick unsalted butter
1 clove garlic, finely chopped
1 tablespoon honey
2 tablespoons soy sauce
1 tablespoon fresh lemon juice

6 salmon fillets, skinless, approximately 6 ounces each

For best results, prepare the salsa 1 hour ahead. In a medium bowl, mix the cucumber, green onion, mint and vinegar. Cover with plastic wrap and chill for 1 hour. Just before serving, stir in the strawberries.

To prepare the barbecue sauce, in a small saucepan, melt butter with garlic over low heat. Stir in the honey, soy sauce and lemon juice and cook for 2 minutes. Set aside.

Prepare a fire in a charcoal grill. When the coals are ready, brush the sauce on the salmon pieces and place in a well-oiled fish-grilling rack. (A grilling rack is not necessary, but it simplifies the cooking and turning of the fish.)

Place the rack over coals about 4 inches from fire and grill approximately 4 to 5 minutes on each side. Brush with the sauce again after turning. (The general rule for cooking fish is that it will take approximately 10 minutes total cooking time for each inch of thickness. Measure the thickest part of the fish fillets to determine the exact total cooking time.)

Baste fish again with barbecue sauce as it finishes cooking. You can tell when the fish is done when it is just barely firm and resilient to the touch.

To serve, open the rack and remove fish fillets with a spatula. Transfer to a warm platter and top with the strawberry, mint and cucumber salsa. *Serves 6*

Broiled Halibut with Greek Lemon Sauce, Huckleberries and Chives

Marinating the firm halibut fillets in lemon and oregano allows the flavors to begin to marry.
The sauce, with more lemon, eggs and a sprinkling of huckleberries and chives, brings the dish to completion.
It's wonderful served with fresh asparagus and little new potatoes.

Marinade:
1/3 cup olive oil
2 tablespoons fresh lemon juice
1 tablespoon coarsely chopped fresh oregano

4 halibut fillets, 3/4- to 1-inch thick
(approximately 6 to 8 ounces each)

Greek Lemon Sauce:
2 tablespoons unsalted butter
2 tablespoons all-purpose flour
1 cup chicken broth, homemade or canned
2 eggs, beaten with 2 tablespoons water
3 tablespoons lemon juice

Salt and freshly ground black pepper, to taste
1 cup huckleberries (or blueberries), for garnish
1 teaspoon chopped fresh chives, for garnish

To prepare the marinade, mix together the olive oil, lemon juice and oregano in a shallow dish. Place halibut fillets in the marinade and refrigerate. Turn fillets after 30 minutes and continue to marinate for another 30 minutes.

To prepare the Greek lemon sauce, melt the butter over low heat in a small saucepan. Stir in the flour. Remove saucepan from heat. Whisk in chicken broth.

Preheat the oven to broil. Broil fillets on a broiler pan or rack 6 inches from heat source, for 4 to 5 minutes per side. Fish should be moist and flake with a fork.

Just before serving, reheat the sauce, then remove from heat and let cool slightly. Stir in beaten eggs and lemon juice. (Be careful that the sauce is cool enough so that the eggs don't scramble.) The mixture will thicken quickly.

Transfer the halibut to a warm serving platter. Season with salt and pepper to taste. Spoon the warm lemon sauce over fish, then sprinkle with huckleberries and chives. *Serves 4*

Chicken with Blackberries, Limes and Fresh Herbs

This tantalizing combination is from Karen Brooks, author of
Oregon's Cuisine of the Rain—From Lush Farm Foods to Regional Recipes.

1 roasting chicken, approximately 4 to 5 pounds
1/4 cup unsalted butter, at room temperature
2 tablespoons chopped fresh sage
3 tablespoons chopped fresh thyme
2 tablespoons chopped fresh rosemary
Zest of 2 lemons, finely chopped
6 cloves garlic, finely chopped
3 tablespoons blackberry preserves

1 tablespoon Dijon mustard
2 tablespoons honey
4 tablespoons soy sauce
Salt and freshly ground black pepper, to taste
2 limes
6 cloves garlic
Sprigs of fresh sage, thyme, rosemary, for garnish
1/2 cup fresh blackberries, for garnish

Preheat the oven to 400 degrees F. Position rack on lowest rungs in the oven.

Wash the chicken thoroughly inside and out and dry with paper towels. Set aside.

In the bowl of a food processor fitted with a steel blade, combine the butter, herbs, lemon zest, chopped garlic, blackberry preserves, mustard, honey and 2 tablespoons of the soy sauce. Blend well and set aside.

Sprinkle the chicken cavity with remaining 2 tablespoons soy sauce and salt and pepper to taste. Prick limes all over with a fork.

Place limes and whole garlic cloves inside chicken cavity. Pull skin at the neck over the opening and skewer closed. Tie legs together with white cotton string.

Rub the exterior of the chicken with salt and pepper. With a pastry brush, brush the chicken with the blackberry-herb mixture. Place chicken on a rack in a roasting pan and place in the oven. Immediately reduce temperature to 375 degrees F. and roast chicken, uncovered, for 10 minutes.

Reduce oven temperature to 350 degrees F. and continue cooking, basting approximately every 15 minutes with pan juices, until the juices run clear when the thigh is pierced, approximately 1 1/2 hours, or 20 minutes per pound of chicken.

Remove skewer and string from chicken. Remove limes and garlic from cavity and discard. Let chicken rest for 10 minutes.

Transfer the chicken to a platter and surround with the fresh sprigs of herbs and fresh blackberries.

Pour the pan juices into a small pan. Let stand for 1 to 2 minutes and skim off any fat that rises to top. Reheat the juices and pour into serving bowl and serve with chicken.
Serves 4

James Beard's Raspberry Chicken

One summer at James Beard's cooking classes in Seaside, Oregon, we had this wonderful chicken dish.
The raspberry vinegar adds a fruity note that complements the chicken well. I find that
cooking the chicken uncovered and over low heat prevents steaming, which can toughen the meat.

4 tablespoons unsalted butter
6 chicken breast halves, rib bones left in,
   skin removed
3 shallots, finely chopped
2/3 cup raspberry vinegar
1 tablespoon tomato paste

2 medium tomatoes, finely chopped
1/2 cup chicken broth, homemade or canned
2 tablespoons unsalted butter
3/4 cup fresh raspberries, for garnish
2 tablespoons chopped chives, for garnish

In a large, heavy-bottomed frying pan, melt the butter over medium heat. Add chicken breasts, meat-side down. Cook uncovered for 5 minutes, until golden brown, then turn the pieces over and cook for an additional 5 minutes. Add the shallots. Turn the heat down slightly and cook for an additional 10 minutes. Transfer chicken to a warm platter.

Pour raspberry vinegar into the frying pan and bring to a boil. Boil for 2 minutes. Turn heat down and stir in the tomato paste, tomatoes and chicken broth. Simmer until sauce thickens slightly. Swirl in 2 tablespoons butter to finish the sauce.

Return chicken pieces to the pan, turning them in the sauce several times to coat well. Cook for 10 minutes on low heat.

Arrange chicken pieces on serving platter and pour sauce over the top. Sprinkle with fresh raspberries and chopped chives. *Serves 6*

Pork Tenderloin with Sautéed Wild Mushrooms, Cranberries, Blueberries and Port

This preparation is the inspiration of Ann and Tony Kischner, owners of the Shoalwater restaurant at the Shelburne Inn where they take advantage of the abundance of edible wild mushrooms growing in the Northwest. Use a combination of wild mushrooms or use commercially grown oyster mushrooms or any other variety you can find at your local grocery store.

1 1/2 sticks unsalted butter, cut into small pieces
1 teaspoon finely chopped garlic
1 1/2 pounds mushrooms, cleaned and sliced 1/4-inch thick
3/4 cup fresh or frozen cranberries (thawing isn't necessary)

6 ounces (approximately 1 cup) fresh or frozen blueberries
1 1/4 cups port wine
Salt and freshly ground black pepper, to taste
2 pork tenderloins, approximately 1 pound each
2 tablespoons olive oil

In a hot sauté pan over medium heat, melt 1 stick of butter with the chopped garlic Add the mushrooms and sauté over medium heat until partially cooked. Add the cranberries, blueberries and port and continue to cook for another 5 minutes, or until mushrooms are soft.

With a slotted spoon, remove the mushrooms, cranberries and blueberries. Set aside on a warm platter.

Preheat the oven to 475 degrees F.

In a sauté pan over high heat, brown the pork in the olive oil. Remove the pork from the pan, sprinkle with the salt and pepper and place on a broiling pan. Do not cover. Bake for 10 minutes.

While the meat is cooking, cook the port sauce over medium-high heat until the liquid is reduced by half. Whisk in remaining butter, bit by bit, until sauce begins to thicken. Return mushrooms and berries to the sauce and heat through until warm.

To serve, slice the pork and top with the sauce. *Serves 6*

Seared Pork Loin with Caramelized Onions and Blackberries

*This dish is an easy supper for 4 people, or for 2 with enough meat
leftover for the next day's sandwiches. It is ideal to make during the month of July
when Walla Walla sweet onions and fresh blackberries are available.*

1 teaspoon granulated sugar
4 tablespoons unsalted butter
2 medium Walla Walla sweet onions
    (or other sweet yellow onions),
    cut in half lengthwise and thinly sliced

1 pork loin roast, approximately 1 1/2 to 2 pounds
Salt and freshly ground black pepper, to taste
1 cup fresh blackberries

Preheat oven to 325 degrees F.

Place the sugar, 2 tablespoons butter and onions into a 9- or 10-inch heavy skillet, over medium heat. Stir onions to coat them with sugar and butter. Cook uncovered for 5 minutes, stirring occasionally.

The onions should turn translucent without coloring. Remove the onions from skillet and set aside.

Melt the remaining butter in the skillet over high heat and brown pork loin on all sides. Transfer the pork loin to a baking pan, sprinkle with the salt and pepper and surround loin with the partially cooked onions. Place the pan in the oven.

Bake in the oven for 1 hour or until the internal temperature reaches from 170 to 180 degrees F. on a meat thermometer. Remove loin from oven and transfer to a warm platter. Surround loin with the caramelized onions and sprinkle the blackberries on top of the hot onions. This goes nicely with new potatoes and peas. *Serves 4*

Marinated Lamb Steaks with Gooseberry Chutney

These tender lamb leg steaks are marinated in a honey-lemon marinade and then broiled or grilled and served with a gooseberry chutney. Made from gooseberries, this versatile chutney is a sweet and savory accompaniment that complements other meats as well.

Marinade:

1 cup extra virgin olive oil
1 tablespoon honey, warmed
1/4 cup fresh lemon juice
2 tablespoons coarsely chopped fresh rosemary
2 cloves garlic, finely chopped

4 lamb leg steaks, cut 1-inch thick

Gooseberry Chutney:

3 cups gooseberries
1 large yellow onion, coarsely chopped
1 1/2 cups light brown sugar
3/4 cup cider vinegar
3/4 cup white wine vinegar
1/2 cup black raisins
1/2 teaspoon ground ginger
1/2 teaspoon turmeric
1/2 teaspoon cayenne pepper
1 teaspoon dry mustard
Kosher salt, to taste

In a small bowl, combine the olive oil, honey, lemon juice, rosemary and garlic. Place lamb steaks in a shallow glass baking dish and pour the marinade over. Refrigerate and marinate for 2 hours.

Remove the stems and blossom nubs from the gooseberries. Rinse and dry well. In a food processor fitted with a steel blade, coarsely chop the gooseberries in 3 batches, transferring each batch to a large saucepan.

Add the chopped onions, brown sugar, vinegars, raisins, ginger, turmeric, cayenne pepper, mustard and a little salt to the pan. Bring to a boil, reduce the heat and simmer for 2 hours, stirring often until chutney is glossy and thickened. *Makes 1 1/2 pints of chutney*

Preheat the oven to broil for at least 5 minutes or prepare an outdoor grill. Broil steaks 3 to 4 inches from the source of heat or cook on an outdoor grill 7 to 10 minutes on each side or until lamb reaches desired degree of doneness. Serve each steak with 2 to 3 spoonfuls of chutney. *Serves 4*

SWEETS

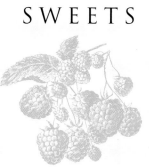

Summer is the perfect time to enjoy tarts, cobblers and pies when berries are flooding the farmers' markets. Berry desserts can be as simple as a dish of fresh raspberries and cream or as elaborate as a beautiful Black, Golden and Red Raspberry Tart. This tart takes time to make, but is worth the effort, especially if you're throwing a special dinner party.

Grunts and crisps are homier baked fruit desserts that have been handed down from the original New England pioneers. The Old-Fashioned Strawberry Rhubarb Grunt has a crumb topping that is baked on top. Willy's Blackberry Crisp is another variation that is easy to assemble and quick to bake.

Chocolate and berries are always a favorite combination. Strawberries dipped in Larry's Chocolate Fudge Sauce will please any chocolate lover. The Chocolate Truffle Pie with Raspberry Sauce will work equally well with frozen raspberries in the winter when fresh berries are no longer available.

For a lighter treat, try layering up a Fourth of July parfait or making your own Strawberry Sorbet. Remember, many of the berries can be substituted for one another in these recipes. Let the berries you find in the market determine what you'll bake tonight.

Black, Golden and Red Raspberry Tart

Fresh fruit tarts are so beautiful, but many times the crust and filling are disappointing.
The wonderful crisp texture of this cornmeal crust and creamy filling will live up to your expectations.

Venetian Cornmeal Crust:
1 1/2 cups all-purpose flour
1 cup fine yellow cornmeal
1/2 teaspoon salt
1 teaspoon baking powder
1 stick unsalted butter, at room temperature
3/4 cup granulated sugar
1/2 teaspoon vanilla extract
1 tablespoon lemon zest

1 whole egg plus 1 egg yolk
1 tablespoon dark rum or water

4 ounces cream cheese, softened
1/4 cup whipping cream
1/3 cup plus 1 tablespoon powdered sugar
1/4 teaspoon vanilla extract
4 ounces fresh mascarpone cheese
*2 cups assorted raspberries (a combination of black,
    golden and red), washed and well dried*

Preheat the oven to 350 degrees F.

In a medium bowl, combine the flour, cornmeal, salt and baking powder. In the bowl of a food processor fitted with a steel blade, place the butter and sugar. Cream until light and fluffy. Add the vanilla, lemon zest, eggs and rum. Pulse until well blended.

Transfer the mixture to the bowl containing the dry ingredients. Stir until well mixed. The dough should be sticky and thick. Wrap in waxed paper. Refrigerate for 30 to 60 minutes.

Divide dough in half (freeze half for another time). Knead the dough 4 to 5 times on a lightly floured surface. Sprinkle a little flour on the dough and the rolling pin to prevent sticking. Roll dough into a 10-inch circle, about 1/4-inch thick. If the dough is sticky, roll out between 2 sheets of waxed paper.

Transfer the dough carefully and place in a 9-inch tart pan with a removable bottom. Lightly press dough into pan. If it tears, simply press it together again.

Cover the dough with aluminum foil and fill with 2 cups of pie weights or uncooked rice or beans. Bake for 20 minutes.

Remove foil and pie weights and bake for an additional 12 minutes, or until the crust browns slightly. Remove from the oven. Let cool for 5 minutes. Carefully remove the outside ring of the pan. With a long metal spatula, gently slip the tart shell off the metal bottom and gently transfer to a cooling rack. Let cool for 30 minutes.

Place cooled tart shell on a serving plate and cover with plastic wrap until ready to fill.

In a large bowl, place cream cheese, whipping cream, powdered sugar and vanilla. Beat until fluffy with an electric mixer. Using a flexible spatula, fold in the mascarpone.

Spread the filling into the cooled tart crust with a flexible spatula. Top filling with black, golden and red raspberries, arranging berries in concentric circles, and refrigerate for 30 minutes. *Serves 6 to 8*

Fourth of July Parfait

This patriotic dessert is beautiful and luscious, celebrating summer
in all its glory. It's sheer berries from top to bottom, layered with creamy clouds
of parfait cream. Parfait cream is a versatile companion for all berries.

Parfait Cream:
8 ounces cream cheese, at room temperature
6 tablespoons powdered sugar
1 cup whipping cream
1 to 2 teaspoons fresh lemon juice, to taste

1 pint fresh blueberries, stemmed and lightly
  sprinkled with sugar
1 pint fresh red raspberries, lightly sprinkled
  with sugar
Fresh mint leaves or lemon balm, for garnish

In a medium bowl, place the cream cheese and powdered sugar. Whip with an electric mixer until fluffy. Slowly add whipping cream a little at a time. Continue beating until the cream is incorporated and mixture is fluffy. Add lemon juice, to taste.

To assemble parfaits, use parfait glasses, tall wine glasses or champagne flutes.

Spoon 1 inch of blueberries into the glass, top with a dollop of cream and then spoon 1 inch of raspberries on top, followed by another dollop of cream. Spoon another layer of blueberries, another dollop of cream and top the parfait with a spoonful of red raspberries. Garnish with mint or lemon balm. *Serves 6 to 8*

Cranberry Clafouti

*A traditional French dessert made with cherries, this variation
of clafouti with cranberries gives it a New England twist.*

3 cups fresh or frozen cranberries
1 1/2 cups cranberry juice or water
6 eggs
1 cup plus 2 tablespoons granulated sugar
6 tablespoons all-purpose flour

1 cup plus 2 tablespoons milk
3/4 cup whipping cream
3/4 teaspoon vanilla extract
1/8 teaspoon ground cinnamon
Whipped cream, for garnish

Preheat the oven to 400 degrees F.

In a heavy saucepan, cook the cranberries in juice or water for 5 minutes over medium-low heat. Strain the berries, reserving the juice, and set the berries aside.

Bring the juice to a boil and continue to cook for approximately 7 minutes, or until the juice is reduced to 1/4 cup.

In the bowl of a food processor or mixer, combine the eggs, sugar, flour, milk, cream and vanilla and mix for approximately 1 minute. Pulse or stir in the reduced juice.

Butter a 9-inch-square baking dish. Spread cranberries over the bottom of the pan. Pour the batter over the berries. Sprinkle with the cinnamon.

Bake for 40 to 45 minutes, or until the top is puffed and golden. Serve hot or warm. Top with whipped cream. *Serves 6*

Old-Fashioned Strawberry Rhubarb Grunt

What a strange name for such an easy, light, delicate-crusted dessert!
I learned this wonderful crust recipe from James Beard years ago and have enjoyed making
it many times. It always brings back fond memories of the very special people
I met and with whom I cooked. It's important to use the right pan for this—a Pyrex
9-inch by 5-inch loaf pan. Metal will react with the acidic rhubarb.

4 cups finely chopped rhubarb
  (approximately 1 1/4 pounds)
1 cup thinly sliced strawberries
3/4 cup granulated sugar
4 tablespoons unsalted butter, cut into small pieces

Crust:
1/4 cup granulated sugar
1 cup self-rising flour
1 cup whipping cream

Vanilla ice cream, for garnish

Preheat oven to 400 degrees F.

In a large bowl, stir the rhubarb and strawberries together and pour into the Pyrex loaf pan. Sprinkle with sugar and dot the top with the butter.

To prepare the crust, mix the sugar and flour in a large bowl. In a small bowl, whip the cream. Gently fold the whipped cream into the sugar and flour mixture. Spread the crust mixture evenly over the fruit.

Bake in the oven for 50 minutes or until filling is bubbly and crust is golden brown. Serve warm topped with vanilla ice cream.
Serves 6

Strawberry Sauce

*This intentionally thick sauce is best used
over other berries or under cake slices.*

*2 cups fresh strawberries, hulled and halved
1/2 cup granulated sugar
1 tablespoon lemon juice or lime juice*

In the bowl of a food processor fitted with a
steel blade, place strawberry halves, sugar and
lemon juice. Process the mixture until it is
smooth and the sugar is dissolved. Serve cool.
Makes approximately 1 1/2 cups. (Refrigerate for
up to 3 days.)

Larry's Chocolate Fudge Sauce

This sauce is heavenly drizzled over fresh berries.

*2/3 cup granulated sugar
1/2 cup unsweetened Dutch process cocoa
3/4 cup whipping cream
1/2 cup light corn syrup
1/8 teaspoon salt
4 ounces unsweetened chocolate, coarsely chopped
5 tablespoons unsalted butter
2 teaspoons vanilla extract*

In a heavy saucepan, combine sugar, cocoa,
cream, corn syrup and salt. Slowly bring to a
boil, stirring to dissolve the sugar. Lower the
heat and simmer for 5 minutes, uncovered. Stir
often. Remove from heat, add chocolate and
butter and stir until melted and smooth. Stir in
vanilla. Serve warm. *Makes approximately 2 cups.*
(Refrigerate for up to 3 weeks. Reheat using
low heat, in a double boiler or microwave.)

Fondant Dipping Sauce

*Fondant is a luxurious dipping sauce for strawberries,
large boysenberries or toasted squares of pound cake.*

*1 cup powdered sugar
1 cup whipping cream
2 tablespoons kirsch or orange curaçao*

In a medium saucepan, combine sugar and
cream. Bring to a vigorous boil, stirring constantly. Remove from heat and stir in liqueur.
Pour into a heat-proof bowl over a candle
warmer and keep warm. *Makes approximately
1 1/2 cups.* (Refrigerate for up to a week.)

Blueberry Sauce

*This rich and tangy sauce is ideal on everything from
breakfast pancakes to your favorite dessert.*

*2 cups fresh or frozen blueberries, (thawed)
1/4 cup orange juice
1/4 cup water
2 tablespoons granulated sugar
1 tablespoon cornstarch
1/4 teaspoon grated orange zest
1/8 teaspoon freshly grated nutmeg
Dash of salt*

In a medium saucepan, combine all the ingredients. Cook over medium heat for 4 to 5
minutes, stirring constantly until the sauce has
thickened. Serve warm. *Makes approximately
2 cups.* (Refrigerate for up to 2 weeks.)

Clockwise, left to right: Larry's Chocolate Fudge Sauce, Fondant Dipping Sauce, Strawberry Sauce and Blueberry Sauce

Chocolate Truffle Pie with Raspberry Sauce and Fresh Raspberries

Sydney Moe, one of my closest friends, loves chocolate. She has made this pie for special occasions many times and everyone loves it. It's very easy and can be made ahead of time.

Crust:
1 1/4 cups graham cracker crumbs
1/4 cup granulated sugar
1 tablespoon unsweetened cocoa
1/2 stick unsalted butter, at room temperature

Filling:
4 ounces semi-sweet chocolate
2 tablespoons milk
8 ounces cream cheese, at room temperature
3 tablespoons granulated sugar

1/3 cup Grand Marnier liqueur
1 3/4 cups whipping cream

Raspberry Sauce:
2 cups fresh raspberries (or two 10-ounce packages frozen sweetened raspberries, thawed)
1/2 cup granulated sugar (for fresh berries only)
1/4 cup Grand Marnier liqueur

1/2 cup whipping cream, whipped
1 tablespoon shaved semi-sweet chocolate
1/2 cup fresh raspberries, for garnish

Preheat the oven to 375 degrees F.

To prepare the crust, mix together graham cracker crumbs, sugar and cocoa in a medium bowl. With a fork, blend in the butter until the mixture has a crumbly consistency.

Using the back of a large spoon, press the crumb mixture firmly inside a 9-inch pie plate to form a crust.

Bake crust in the oven for 8 minutes. Remove and let cool.

To prepare the filling, melt the chocolate with milk over low heat in a small saucepan, stirring constantly. Let cool.

In a large bowl, beat the cream cheese and sugar together. Add the Grand Marnier and melted chocolate mixture and blend. Do not overmix. Whip the cream in a small bowl and fold into the chocolate mixture. Pour the mixture into the cooled crust and spread evenly with a spatula. Cover with plastic wrap and refrigerate overnight.

The next day, prepare the raspberry sauce. Using a food processor fitted with a steel blade, purée the fresh berries or thawed frozen berries. Strain out the seeds. If you are using fresh berries, add the sugar and pulse to dissolve the sugar. Add the Grand Marnier and mix until the sauce is blended.

Top the pie with the whipped cream, shaved chocolate and fresh raspberries. Serve with the raspberry sauce. *Serves 6 to 8*

Willie's Blackberry Crisp

In the Northwest we have 2 varieties of wild blackberries. One we seek out and the other seeks us out—and threatens to take over our garden every year. Both varieties are delicious, they just lend themselves to different uses. The small, coast trailing blackberry, with its sweet-tart flavor, is prized for cobblers, pies and jams. The large Himalayan, which is juicy and seedy, is best in crisps, jellies, spritzer base and vinegars. This recipe is a good way to use the larger berries that are so abundant.

Crust Topping:
1 cup all-purpose flour
1 cup granulated sugar
1 teaspoon baking powder
1 egg, beaten

Blackberry Filling:
2 tablespoons all-purpose flour
3/4 cup granulated sugar
4 to 5 cups fresh or frozen blackberries

1 stick unsalted butter, melted

Preheat the oven to 375 degrees F.

In a medium bowl, combine the flour, sugar and baking powder. Make a well in the center of the dry ingredients and blend in the egg, mixing until the topping is crumbly. Set aside.

To prepare the filling, mix the flour and sugar in a small bowl. Place the blackberries in a large bowl and sprinkle with the flour and sugar mixture. Toss gently to evenly coat the blackberries.

Transfer berry mixture to a well-buttered 8-inch by 8-inch by 2-inch glass baking dish and sprinkle topping over berries.

Drizzle melted butter evenly over the crumbly topping. Place baking dish on a baking sheet to prevent spillovers into the oven. Bake for 45 minutes. *Serves 6*

Black Lake Blueberry Deep-Dish Pie

*At Black Lake, Washington, we have good friends who have a large blueberry patch. This is
their summer specialty whenever there is a gathering at their home. It is so easy. You can even use fresh or
frozen berries. The addition of the apple to the filling gives a little substance to the juicy berries.*

Pastry for a double-crust, 10-inch pie (see page 80)

Filling:
4 cups fresh or frozen blueberries, unthawed
1 Golden Delicious apple,
    peeled and coarsely chopped
1/2 cup granulated sugar

1 tablespoon cornstarch
2 to 3 tablespoons unsalted butter,
    cut into small pieces
1/2 teaspoon ground cinnamon

1 teaspoon granulated sugar
Vanilla ice cream

Prepare the crust and place lower crust in a 10-inch glass deep-dish pie plate or a 9-inch-square baking pan.

Preheat the oven to 425 degrees F.

To prepare the filling, mix the blueberries and apple with the sugar and cornstarch. Spoon the filling into the crust-lined pie plate or baking pan.

Dot the top with butter pieces. Sprinkle with cinnamon and drape the upper crust over the buttered berries. Trim and crimp the edges closed. Cut several steam vents in the crust.

Sprinkle top of crust with additional sugar. Bake in the oven for 25 minutes. Serve warm with vanilla ice cream. *Serves 6 to 8*

Bumbleberry Pie

Bumbleberry pie is an old-fashioned name for a pie made with
several varieties of berries. In the middle of July, when raspberries, boysenberries,
blackberries and blueberries are all available, I like to make this pie.

Pastry for a double-crust, 10-inch pie (see page 80)

Filling:
1 3/4 cups granulated sugar
4 tablespoons arrowroot
3 cups fresh red raspberries

1 cup fresh boysenberries
1 1/2 cups fresh blackberries,
    preferably the small wild variety
1 1/2 cups fresh blueberries
2 tablespoons unsalted butter, cut into small pieces

Prepare the pastry and place lower crust in a 10-inch pie pan.

Preheat oven to 425 degrees F.

In a large bowl, combine the sugar and arrowroot, then gently toss with the berries. (If you are using frozen berries, thaw, drain the berries and increase amount of arrowroot by 1 to 2 tablespoons.)

Let the filling mixture stand for a few minutes, then spoon into the pie shell and dot with butter. Gently place the top crust over the berries and crimp the edges together with your thumb and forefinger. Use a sharp knife to make small slashes in the top crust to allow steam to escape. Or for a fancier presentation, make a lattice crust. Bake for 25 minutes. Reduce heat to 350 degrees F. and bake for an additional 35 minutes.

The pie will be done when juices start to bubble slightly out of the steam cuts. *Serves 8*

Double-Crust for 10-Inch Pie

The cake flour is the secret in this crust recipe. It makes the crust extremely tender.
I have found that using shortening for berry pie crusts prevents soggy pies.

2 cups cake flour
2/3 cup chilled shortening

1/2 teaspoon salt
6 tablespoons ice water

Place the cake flour in a medium bowl. Add the shortening and salt. With the tips of your fingers or using a pastry blender, rub the flour and shortening together until well blended. (This only takes a few minutes.)

Sprinkle in the ice water, stirring with a fork. Gather the dough together with your hands, forming a ball. Divide the dough in half. Flatten into two 5-inch rounds, approximately 1/2 inch thick.

Wrap dough with plastic wrap and chill approximately 45 minutes to 1 hour. Dough can be frozen until further use. Thaw at room temperature.

Marionberry Peach Crunch

The combination of tart berries and sweet peaches in this easy-to-assemble dish makes it
a favorite for everyone—including the cook. I like to make a double batch of topping and keep half
of it in the freezer for the next crunch. It's good for breakfast as well as dessert.

Crunch Topping:
1 cup steel-cut rolled oats
1 cup all-purpose flour
1/2 teaspoon ground cinnamon
1/2 cup dark brown sugar
1 stick margarine or unsalted butter
1 cup chopped pecans (optional)

Fruit Filling:
3 cups (approximately 1 pound) sliced fresh peaches,
  cut in 1/2-inch-thick slices
3 cups marionberries
3/4 cup granulated sugar
2 tablespoons all-purpose flour

Vanilla ice cream, for garnish

Preheat the oven to 350 degrees F.

To prepare the crunch topping, combine the oats, flour, cinnamon and brown sugar in a medium bowl. With your fingers, blend in the butter, until the topping is crumbly. Add the pecans, if desired, and set aside.

To prepare the fruit filling, mix the peaches and berries with sugar and flour, coating the fruit well in a medium bowl. Spoon the filling into a 6-inch by 9-inch glass baking dish. Spread crunch topping evenly over fruit. Bake in the oven for 1 hour or until the top is a golden brown color and the fruit is bubbling.

Serve warm with vanilla ice cream. This also makes a nice breakfast treat topped with a little cream or yogurt. *Serves 6*

Strawberry Sorbet

This frozen refreshment is perfect for summertime.
You don't even need to have an ice cream maker to make it.

Sugar Syrup:
3/4 cup granulated sugar
3/4 cup water

4 cups strawberries, hulled and halved
1/2 cup orange juice

Juice of 1/2 lemon
1/4 cup raspberry liqueur, for garnish
6 whole strawberries, for garnish
Mint leaves, for garnish

To prepare the sugar syrup, combine the sugar and water in a medium saucepan. Bring to a boil, then simmer for 10 minutes. Let cool, then refrigerate.

Place strawberries and orange juice in a food processor fitted with a steel blade, and pulse until mixture is smooth. Add the 1 1/2 cups of sugar syrup and lemon juice.

Pour the sorbet mixture into a 9-inch by 13-inch cake pan. Cover with plastic wrap and place in the freezer and freeze until slushy, approximately 1 hour.

Return to a food processor fitted with a steel blade and process until smooth.

Return the sorbet to the cake pan, cover with plastic wrap and freeze until firm, approximately 2 hours.

To serve, use a large spoon and scoop the sorbet into small ice cream dishes. Top with a little raspberry liqueur and garnish with fresh strawberries and mint leaves. *Serves 6*

BEVERAGES

When berries are in season, they provide endless possibilities for homemade beverages, great for any time of the day. The Strawberry Pineapple Smoothie is a nutritious breakfast drink and a source of quick energy in the afternoon.

When I entertain in the evening, I always offer my guests something to drink before dinner. Cool summer drinks made with berries are just a delight to make.

Mel's Black Currant Cooler relies on the use of the berry liqueur crème de cassis, while the Blackberry Spritzer employs freshly puréed berries. Both are drinks with lots of fizz that will awaken anyone's appetite.

For a more powerful punch, the classic Strawberry Daiquiri is a great way to beat the heat. If you feel like being adventuresome, you can always substitute a more exotic berry for the strawberries. In the Strawberry Margarita recipe, the traditional cocktail gets a face-lift with the addition of beer, inspired by a recipe some good friends shared with me after discovering this variation in New Mexico. Making your own fruit-flavored vodka can also be fun, and the Raspberry Liqueur recipe shows you just how easy it is.

Berry Ice Cubes in Sparkling Water (recipe p. 86)

Raspberry Liqueur

The bright red color and fresh flavor of this home-made flavored vodka will enhance soda spritzers or champagne. It's also terrific on broiled grapefruit.

1 pound raspberries
1 pound granulated sugar
1 fifth vodka

Mix all the ingredients in a 1-gallon, wide-mouthed jar. Store in a cool, dark place. Stir or shake every few days for about 3 weeks.

Strain through several layers of cheese-cloth, reserving the liquid, but discarding the pulp and seeds.

Refrigerated, the liqueur will keep indefinitely. *Makes approximately 5 cups*

Mel's Black Currant Cooler

Tall, cool and sparkling, with a European accent, this sophisticated beverage can be enjoyed by people at all ages.

4 ice cubes
1 1/2 ounces crème de cassis (also known as
black currant syrup or sirop de cassis)
5 to 6 ounces cold ginger ale
Mint leaves, for garnish

Fill a tall glass with ice cubes. Pour the crème de cassis over the ice. Fill the glass with ginger ale, garnish with a mint sprig and serve. *Serves 1*

Berry Ice Cubes

Any type of whole, ripe berries, such as blueberries, raspberries or blackberries (except strawberries)

Fill ice cube trays with 1 or 2 berries in each section. Cover with water and freeze over-night. Add to your favorite beverage as you would a regular ice cube.

Mel's Black Currant Cooler

Left to right: Strawberry Daiquiri and Strawberry Margarita

Strawberry Daiquiri

*On a perfect summer evening, put your
gardening tools down, put your feet up on a footstool
and sip a refreshing strawberry daiquiri.*

6 ounces limeade or lemonade concentrate, thawed
2 1/2 cups sliced strawberries
1 tablespoon granulated sugar
6 ounces rum
3 to 4 cups ice
6 whole strawberries, for garnish

Place the limeade, strawberries, sugar and rum
in a blender. Fill the blender with ice cubes.
Blend until mixture is smooth. Pour daiquiris
into 6 glasses and garnish each serving with a
fresh, ripe strawberry. *Serves 6*

Strawberry Margarita

*Here's another twist on a refreshing
summer cooler. Yes, it really does call for beer,
which blends all the flavors together.*

6 ounces frozen limeade concentrate, thawed
6 ounces beer
6 ounces tequila
2 cups ice cubes
2 cups sliced strawberries
Thin lime slices and whole strawberries, for garnish

Place the limeade, beer, tequila, ice cubes and
sliced strawberries in a blender. Whirl until the
ice is crushed. Pour into 4 large wine glasses
and garnish with lime slices and strawberries.
Serves 4

Blackberry Spritzer

*Blackberry syrup base is just the ticket
for summer spritzers. You can also use it in sodas,
milkshakes, punches or other beverages.*

Blackberry Syrup Base:
8 cups fresh or frozen blackberries
1 cup granulated sugar or to taste

3 cups blackberry base
3 cups sparkling soda water
Lemon twists, for garnish (optional)
Ice cubes

To make the blackberry syrup base, place the blackberries in a food processor fitted with a steel blade, and pulse until partly puréed.

In a saucepan, heat the berry purée to a boil, then simmer about 5 minutes until juice is released.

Place a sieve over a bowl and pour in the berry purée. Gently press the juice through the sieve with a wooden spoon, until only the seeds remain.

Return berry juice to the saucepan. Add sugar, to taste. Bring to a boil and cook until sugar is dissolved.

Let mixture cool, pour into a quart jar, cover and refrigerate. The base can be stored in the refrigerator for a month. *Makes 3 cups*

To make a blackberry spritzer, fill 6 glasses with ice. Pour 1/2 cup blackberry base into each glass. Fill glasses with sparkling water and serve with lemon twist, if desired. *Serves 6*

Strawberry Pineapple Smoothie

*Sometimes you want something to
drink that's fresh tasting and filling, but not heavy
and rich. This smoothie is it.*

1/2 cup fresh pineapple chunks
1 cup strawberries (fresh or frozen), halved or sliced
1 banana, peeled and sliced into 1/2-inch pieces
2 cups buttermilk
1 to 2 tablespoons honey
3 to 4 fresh mint leaves
4 ice cubes
Fresh strawberries or pineapple chunks, for garnish

Place all the ingredients except the garnish in a blender and purée until smooth. Pour into 4 tall glasses and garnish with a strawberry or a pineapple chunk cut 3/4 of the way through and perched on the lip of the glass. *Serves 4*

METRIC CONVERSIONS

Liquid Weights

U.S. Measurements	Metric Equivalents
1/4 teaspoon	1.23 ml
1/2 teaspoon	2.5 ml
3/4 teaspoon	3.7 ml
1 teaspoon	5 ml
1 dessertspoon	10 ml
1 tablespoon (3 teaspoons)	15 ml
2 tablespoons (1 ounce)	30 ml
1/4 cup	60 ml
1/3 cup	80 ml
1/2 cup	120 ml
2/3 cup	160 ml
3/4 cup	180 ml
1 cup (8 ounces)	240 ml
2 cups (1 pint)	480 ml
3 cups	720 ml
4 cups (1 quart)	1 litre
4 quarts (1 gallon)	3 3/4 litres

Dry Weights

U.S. Measurements	Metric Equivalents
1/4 ounce	7 grams
1/3 ounce	10 grams
1/2 ounce	14 grams
1 ounce	28 grams
1 1/2 ounces	42 grams
1 3/4 ounces	50 grams
2 ounces	57 grams
3 ounces	85 grams
3 1/2 ounces	100 grams
4 ounces (1/4 pound)	114 grams
6 ounces	170 grams
8 ounces (1/2 pound)	227 grams
9 ounces	250 grams
16 ounces (1 pound)	464 grams

Temperatures

Farenheit	Celsius (Centigrade)
32°F (water freezes)	0°C
200°F	95°C
212°F (water boils)	100°C
250°F	120°C
275°F	135°C
300°F (slow oven)	150°C
325°F	160°C
350°F (moderate oven)	175°C
375°F	190°C
400°F (hot oven)	205°C
425°F	220°C
450°F (very hot oven)	230°C
475°F	245°C
500°F (extremely hot oven)	260°C

Length

U.S. Measurements	Metric Equivalents
1/8 inch	3 mm
1/4 inch	6 mm
3/8 inch	1 cm
1/2 inch	1.2 cm
3/4 inch	2 cm
1 inch	2.5 cm
1 1/4 inches	3.1 cm
1 1/2 inches	3.7 cm
2 inches	5 cm
3 inches	7.5 cm
4 inches	10 cm
5 inches	12.5 cm

Approximate Equivalents

1 kilo is slightly more than 2 pounds

1 litre is slightly more than 1 quart

1 meter is slightly over 3 feet

1 centimeter is approximately 3/8 inch

INDEX